THE BEGINNING PROFESSIONAL WRITER

BUSINESS FOR BREAKFAST, VOLUME 1

LEAH R CUTTER

KNOTTED ROAD PRESS

ALSO BY LEAH R CUTTER

The Shadow Wars Trilogy
The Raven and the Dancing Tiger
The Guardian Hound
War Among the Crocodiles

The Clockwork Fairy Kingdom
The Clockwork Fairy Kingdom
The Maker, the Teacher, and the Monster
The Dwarven Wars

Seattle Trolls
The Changeling Troll
The Princess Troll
The Fairy-Bridge Troll

Contemporary Fantasy
The Immortals' War
Siren's Call

The Cassie Stories
Poisoned Pearls
Tainted Waters
Spoiled Harvest

The Chronicles of Franklin

The Popcorn Thief

The Soul Thief

FOREWARD BY BLAZE WARD

I've learned a lot from Leah since I took up the Craft. How to write better. How to tell better stories (not the same thing). How to think like a professional writer. When she starts talking to other writers, she's bringing years of experience as a technical writer, programmer, and nerd to the table.

Many of the writers I know are extremely experienced and knowledgeable about the craft of writing, far more than I will ever accomplish. But rarely have the stepped very far outside of their shell of being a writer. When they do, they confront a world where all (ALL) of the old assumptions about how to be a professional writer have been completely upended.

Those of you with the right historical bent will understand that we are living through what Joseph Schumpeter described in manufacturing and capitalism, where the forces of modernization, in their relentlessly impersonal way, continuously innovate forward. The term is 'Creative Destruction.'

Schumpeter's Gale levels everything. It has arrived on our shores. What used to be TradPub fifty years ago is gone.

Today, you have to come face to face with a world where you are your own business manager. My musician friends and family are a decade ahead of us in having to be all things to all people in their career. But you do not have to go it alone.

What Leah has done is taken all the complicated lessons she had to learn over the last few years and boiled them down into easy-to-understand, bite-sized morsels and in language geared toward the professional writer. You can go from just being a writer to being a product, and understanding why you are doing what you do. I know future books will cover other things, including how to turn yourself into a small-press publisher if you choose, on understanding how they work so you can protect yourself against being taken advantage of.

It has already made me a better writer to know these things. I am looking forward to what comes next. I think you will also benefit, because up until now, did you even know what questions you needed to ask?

Blaze Ward
January 2015

PUBLISHER'S NOTE BY URSULA LEIGHTON

This books is the one hundredth title that Knotted Road Press (KRP) has published.

Not the first business book, and certainly not the first non-fiction book that I've done.

The first non-fiction book was a charming autobiography by Terry Brodbeck Ward. She'd grown up on a carnival in the 1930s and '40s, in mid-west America. It was a collection of memories from a time in America that has rapidly disappeared, a time when a small town's entertainment for the year was the traveling carnival, a time before TV.

The book is merely a chapbook, perhaps 40 pages long. It's something that only a small press like KRP would pick up.

Does it have a large readership? No.

Does it have a readership? Absolutely.

And that's one of the best things about being the publisher for KRP in this day in age. Instead of trying to create an audience, or generate velocity, or even buzz, I can publish a book and trust that the readers who are looking for that kind of work will find it.

I get to trust the readers.

While this may only be KRP's hundredth title, it won't be too long before there's two hundred books, then three hundred.

As Business for Breakfast discusses, some of those titles will only ever be drips: a sale here, a sale there.

But those drips will combine into trickles.

Some titles will be trickles on their own. And hopefully, at some point, streams.

It's a wonderful time to be publishing and to be able to take the long view.

I hope that you'll enjoy taking this journey with us.

Ursula Leighton
Publisher, Knotted Road Press

INTRODUCTION BY LEAH CUTTER

This book is designed for the artist/writer, the creative type. I will use terms and concepts that I, as an artist/writer, understand better than the business terms that the rest of the world uses.

In addition, although I think of myself as an artist, this book is primarily for the writer who is just starting and is in their first few years of seriously writing. It's to help you start becoming a professional writer. I define a *professional writer* as someone who is interested in earning money, possibly all their income, from their writing.

I've always intended to be a professional writer, to earn all my income from my writing. My first novel was published by Roc (a New York publisher) back in 2003 (yes, the dark ages). My next two novels were published in succeeding years, 2004 and 2005.

Things happened then, as they do in any career, and I stopped writing and publishing for about five years.

Meanwhile, the indie revolution happened.

I published my first ebook in 2011. And I've never looked back.

For twenty-odd years, I supported my writing habit with a day job. I did technical writing. I became an expert at translating programmer-ese into English.

In 2014, I went to the Advanced Master Publishing workshop. It occurred to me, talking with the writers there, that my expertise in translating could be useful to other writers. However, instead of translating computer-related things, I could translate business-ese into artist-ese.

When Dean Wesley Smith came up with the title for this series, *Business for Breakfast*, it all fell into place.

Why did he suggest that name?

In 2013, I went to a different workshop about publishing. It was a week long. It spent an entire day on corporations: S-corp and C-corp and company structures, etc.

I knew *nothing* about corporations. In addition, the instructors used a lot of business terms that were completely unfamiliar to me.

And yet, I consider myself a something of a business person. I run three successful small businesses:

- Fiction writer
- Small press publisher
- Vacation rental owner

I knew I needed to educate myself on these terms if I wanted to continue to grow my writing and publishing businesses.

So I bought one of those big business books from NOLO press. You know the ones. The huge tomes that are pretty much a guaranteed cure for insomnia.

I knew that sitting down and trying to read something like that from start to finish was impossible. Expecting myself to do that was guaranteeing failure.

Instead, I made it a habit to read this book in chunks. Twenty minutes, every morning, while I ate breakfast.

Doing that, I was able to get through the momentous tome of *Incorporate Your Business: A Legal Guide to Forming a Corporation in Your State*. As well as *The Copyright Handbook: What Every Writer Needs to Know*. And *The Freelancer's Survival Guide*.

NOTE: See the recommended reading list in the Appendix.

This book is also designed to be digested in very small chunks. None of the chapters are longer than 1300 words. You can read each one in twenty minutes or less. Perhaps over breakfast. Thus, the name of this book and this series.

By the end of this book, my goal is to have given you, the

artist/writer, enough information such that you understand what it means to be a professional business person. How much of this information that you use is up to you. Your business, as well as your career, will be different than mine. You have your own choices to make.

There are many paths to the mountain. This book will help you figure out the right equipment for you.

I hope to see you around the breakfast table.

Leah Cutter
January 2015

CHAPTER ONE

Breaking Up Is Hard To Do

Writing is a great, great thing. And it may be all you've focused on until now.

However, your *writing* is not the same as your *business*.

Even before money gets involved, you must start thinking about your business, not just your writing.

This chapter is all about separating you, the artist/writer, from your business.

As a writer, you're familiar with having different voices, people, characters in your head.

Your business is just one more separate entity. Another voice you'll need to learn about and use.

Doing Business As (DBA)

DBA stands for Doing Business As. It may or may not be called that in your state or country. For example, in Washington state, it's called *trade name*. In Idaho, it's called a *business license*. In California, it's called a *Fictitious Business Name*.

Do you need a DBA? Unfortunately, the answer is, it depends. Not just on your intention, but your state and country.

If you are going to be publishing your work, you probably need a DBA for your publishing house. (Again, check your state or country laws.)

If you are submitting your work to publishers, you may or may not need one, depending on your state or country's banking laws.

Why do you need a DBA?

Because this is part of the breaking apart of you and your business.

Businesses have their own separate checking accounts. Their own separate credit cards. Their own separate accounting.

In Washington state, I needed a DBA in order to open up separate checking accounts for my businesses.

In your state or country, you may also need a DBA to open up separate banking accounts for both your writing business and your publishing business.

The Whys

Why do you need a separate checking account?

To make it easier to keep track of both income and expenses.

But I don't have any income yet!

That may be true today. It may be true a year from now.

Will it still be true five years from now? Ten years from now?

You are setting up the structure now, so that when you do start making money, everything will be in place and you won't be scrambling or in a panic.

Which means I can do this a year from now, right?

There's another reason why you want to separate your writing from your business, and to do it sooner rather than later. *Before* you start earning income.

Taxes

First of all, the disclaimer: I am not a tax professional, nor do I play one on TV. I cannot actually give you tax advice.

All I can do is to make you aware of some things.

Even if you don't care about saving money on your taxes, you should still understand the following principles.

In the United States, as your business, you are generally what is called a *sole proprietor*. This means that on your taxes, you'll fill out something called a Schedule C.

I know. I know. Deep breaths. It'll be okay. I'm not about to get into the nitty-gritty of something like a Schedule C. You'll need to talk to a tax professional about that.

All I'm here to tell you about is that, for the business of an artist/writer, a Schedule C may help you save money.

How?

By possibly lowering your taxable income.

(Notice all the weasel words in these statements. *May. Possibly.* Again, not giving you advice or guaranteeing you anything. Please don't sue me.)

In the United States, one of the things that the Internal Revenue Service (IRS) looks at is whether your writing is a business or a hobby.

From their guidelines:

Generally, an activity qualifies as a business if it is carried on with the reasonable expectation of earning a profit.

Are you submitting your work? If the answer is *yes*, you have the reasonable expectation of earning a profit.

If you're publishing it yourself, the answer to that is *yes* as well.

You must keep a record of your submissions as well as what you publish. That is enough to show to the IRS that your intention is to make money.

With that record, you are a business, not a hobby.

Three-Year-Profit Nonsense

Again, not giving you tax advice here. You need to make your own choice and decision.

There's a lot of misinformation about "you must show a profit three years out of five."

How long did Amazon.com go without showing a profit? Ten years? Twelve years? Are they even making a profit yet?

3

Yet no one would accuse them of being a hobby and not a business.

There is a difference between *profit* and *income*. I devote a whole chapter to it later.

If you're worried that the IRS may think of your writing business as a hobby, there are plenty of ways to demonstrate your *intent*. For example, creating a website for your publisher. Having an Amazon Author page with all of your independently published books listed. Maybe even registering as a DBA and having separate checking accounts for your writing business.

All of these things show the intent to make money.

Which makes you a business.

Not whether you show a profit or not.

Deductions

I am not a Certified Public Accountant (CPA) nor do I ever want to play one on TV. All I can do is tell you about things I've learned. I'm not giving you advice.

Why should you keep good records, keep track of everything?

So you can deduct *legal* expenses off your taxes.

Why do you care about that?

You pay taxes on your income.

Your expenses are subtracted from your income.

Lower income can mean lower taxes.

The IRS has lists of what count as business expenses, including but not limited to:

- Advertising expenses
- Education expenses
- Internet-related expenses
- Subscriptions

So look at this list from your writing business point of view.

You take a workshop or a class about writing. That is an Education expense.

This is a business expense, that you can then deduct from your taxable income.

You write about horses. You've published short stories or novels about horses. You subscribe to *Horse Lover's Monthly* magazine. This is a Subscription.

This is a business expense.

You purchase your own domain name. The domain registration fees are an Internet expense.

This is a business expense.

By subtracting your expenses from your income, you may lower your taxes.

In Conclusion

The three things you need to remember:

- Separate yourself from your business, so that you can more easily keep track of expenses and show intent to operate as a business.
- Keep good records of your intent to be a business (submitting or publishing your writing) as well as your expenses.
- Intent is key. Not income.

CHAPTER TWO

Property

For your writing business, what do you create?

I know, I know. Stories. Novels. Worlds. Intergalactic government plots. Descriptions of pure love that leave your readers in tears.

All of that may be true.

But those are all the *writing* side of that creation.

What do you create in terms of the business?

This chapter describes the concept of *intellectual property*, as well as introduces some of the important concepts around copyright.

Copyright, The Beginning

First of all, I recommend that you read *The Copyright Handbook* from NOLO Press.

Yes, it's a huge tome. Maybe alternate your reading of it with this book and tackle it twenty minutes at a time.

I know a writer who opens that book at random once a week, when she has a couple of hours to spare. She'll find a specific aspect of copyright that interests her, then she'll do a deep dive of that topic to thoroughly understand it.

Whatever your method, as an artist/writer, you *must* understand copyright. This is not something you can pass off to your business partner or agent.

Let me put it this way, when you "sell" a story, what exactly are you selling?

For your business, how can you sell something if you don't know what it is you're selling?

The Subdivision

Kudos to Dean Wesley Smith for coming up with the subdivision metaphor.

When you make the decision to start writing, you have just sectioned off a subdivision; that is, a large piece of land on which you are about to build houses, flats, and parks.

Every time you write a short story or a novel, you are building a house in that subdivision.

If you write many books in a series, you might want to think about it as developing a neighborhood in that subdivision.

A building, on a lot, is a physical piece of property.

Every story or novel you create is also property, but it's called *intellectual* property.

In many ways, intellectual property is treated identically to physical property.

When you "sell" a short story or a novel to a publisher, are you actually selling the property?

No.

(That is, not if you're smart and you haven't signed away all your rights in the contract. But going into depth about contracts is beyond the scope of this book. It may be covered in detail in a future *Business for Breakfast* volume.)

What you are doing is *licensing rights* to the publisher for a specific amount of time.

The publisher pays you for that license.

They do *not* own the property.

They are merely renting a particular house in your subdivision.

Again, watch your contracts to make sure that they can't make changes to that house without your written approval. (These are often referred to as *moral rights*.) A bad contract could let someone else completely rewrite your material without your approval or review.

You also need to be aware of competition clauses in contracts, so that you can continue to build similar houses in that subdivision or neighborhood.

Apartment Buildings (or Flats)

To continue with the metaphor, sometimes instead of an individual house, you end up constructing a larger building with many individual rooms inside of it for rent.

Only one person can rent a single room at a time.

But all of those rooms can be rented.

That is, you can *individually* license the audio rights, German language rights, screenplay rights, T-shirt printing rights, roleplaying game rights, etc.

Each of those *forms* of your work is an individual room you can rent in that one property.

Again, watch your contracts. Make sure that you're not giving away the entire building when you sign a contract.

Form

Copyright is based on the *form* of the work. That is, once you commit a work to a format, such as when you save an electronic file, it is automatically copyrighted.

NOTE: There are some exceptions to this. Recent court cases have not accepted backups to a cloud as being copyrighted. Print is still king.

This means that the copyright for an electronic work is separate for the copyright for a printed work, etc.

It is no longer required that you must specify **Copyright © by XXX DATE.** For a few years, back in the 1980s, it was. If that attribution was accidentally left off of your book, the material automatically entered public domain.

However, it's still a good idea.

And remember, you're copyrighting the *form*.

When you create a print book, you can specify the following:

Interior design copyright © by XXX DATE

Registration

In the United States, you can also *register* your copyright. There are other conventions in other parts of the world to accomplish the same thing—you'll need to look up what is legal where you live.

Registering your work is different than merely copyrighting your material.

The difference has to do with how the courts treat your work if someone tries to steal it, which is also called *infringing*.

You can claim statutory damages if your work is registered.

In the United States, this means that the court can fine the person who has stolen your work for *every* copy produced.

For example, if the person who stole your work produced an electronic copy, and thousands of copies were purchased, the court could charge them for *every single copy* that was sold, between $750 to $30,000 per copy.

Does it makes sense to register every single piece of work you produce?

Probably not. It costs money and takes time.

When should you register your copyright?

My rule of thumb is to register longer works (i.e., novels) and any property that I think is an office building, not a simple house.

That is, if I think a property has more than one room I can easily license, I'll register the copyright.

In the United States, the site for registering your copyright is: https://copyright.gov/registration/

Signing Away Rights

You can only *sign away* your copyright.

There must be a signed agreement between the parties.

HOWEVER.

The courts have accepted the Terms of Service agreements, the online kind that nobody except copyright geeks like me read as *signed agreements*.

You might want to start paying attention to those agreements before you automatically scroll to the bottom and click "I agree."

In addition, in the United States, at this time, the *only* place where verbal agreements are legally binding are in California.

So be careful if you're talking on the phone with someone from Hollywood. There are unscrupulous people out there. They might claim at a later date that the twenty-minute conversation you had about your cats was actually when you verbally told them they could produce your work for nothing, that you verbally gave them your copyright.

In Conclusion

These are the three things you need to remember about property:

- In many ways, intellectual property is treated the same way as physical property. Every story or novel you create is another house in your subdivision.
- Copyright is by *form*, which you can specifically register for greater protection against someone stealing (infringing) your work.
- You can only sign away your copyright.

CHAPTER THREE

Drips to Trickles to Streams

Why you write or create art probably has nothing to do with money.

Why you publish may or may not have anything to do with money.

And possibly there is no money coming in at this point.

But your *intent* is to make money by licensing your art.

This chapter describes how that happens for many artists, and how to think about the money coming in during this new age of publishing.

Drips

Suppose you write a short story and decide to publish it yourself. Somebody buys it. Great!

This is a drip.

You make another sale that month. Maybe you don't sell anything the following month. Then you have another sale.

Many properties (remember, every story or novel is intellectual property, and can be referred to as property) work in this fashion.

A sale here, a sale there.

Of course, you could always bottle lightning. Hit the social zeitgeist. Sell a million copies of the very first novel you put up.

Those are the exceptions.

For most artists, the first pieces generate drips and nothing more.

Trickles

Everyone who has read your stuff loves it. You continue to write and publish. But your work hasn't found its audience yet.

Drips continue.

Then, at some point, maybe after your tenth or twentieth novel, you notice a change.

A single property may still only have a sale every other month or so.

However, this second property is also selling a copy every other month. And that third property as well. And maybe there are a couple of other properties that sell that way.

Not a single property is selling consistently or well.

However, all of your properties sell one or two here or there.

Suddenly, you have a trickle. Instead of a single sale of a single property, you have a single sale of a dozen different properties.

This is a trickle. It isn't enough to live on. May only be coffee money.

But it's a constant trickle of money.

Streams

So you continue to write and publish. You've continued to improve your property. Maybe you've spruced up a neighborhood by painting the houses—that is, putting new covers on your work. Or you've taken a class and learned how to write great blurbs and have updated those.

Now you catch the attention of a voracious reader, who goes through and buys everything you've written.

You're going to get reviews. Nothing that you've paid for, but from fans who genuinely like your work.

You're selling more copies. Maybe you sell a short story to a major magazine or to an anthology.

Your income jumps to the next level. Suddenly, instead of just trickles, those trickles have combined to become a stream.

But that's just a single stream—your published electronic work.

You now need to add more streams. Like print books. And audio. And hey, you have a friend who's an artist who's always wanted to illustrate one of your books. So you do a graphic novel.

Or maybe you've only ever written fiction, but you know a lot about business. So you start writing and publishing non-fiction.

Instead of a single stream of money coming in, you have many streams.

Rivers

If you continue to play the long game, the slow game, then eventually you'll get there. Maybe a book will take off after you've written twenty, and you'll be an "overnight success" after years of hard work.

Or maybe for your career, you'll just combine all those streams into a river.

Professional writers, those with long careers, all have seen this sort of ebb and flow of money. Money washes in, then they go through a dry spell, then it flows again.

You should expect the same thing of your long-term career as well. Things change. They always do. New technology occurs. New stores pop open and close.

Streams dry up. But then they come roaring back with new life.

Have many streams flowing into your rivers.

Have many neighborhoods filled with different types of houses in your subdivision.

Money

Money is always an interesting concept. Most people won't talk about it, not in specifics.

But we all have ideas about money, where it comes from, how

hard it is to acquire.

I know more than one artist that have unconsciously sabotaged themselves by not understanding themselves.

It has nothing to do with being good or bad with money. That's the end result.

As an artist, you need to dig deeper.

In your family of origin, what were their attitudes toward money?

Were you raised to believe that money is something you'll never have? Or were you raised to believe that money will just always come in, whether you work or not? Or perhaps you were raised to think money should never be associated with your art?

Your underlying attitudes toward money will affect your drips and trickles and streams and rivers.

If you think you can never have money—that money will never come to you—you'll stop writing and publishing, won't believe the constant drips, and will take your work down when you start selling. (I've seen it happen.)

Or you stop working because you've put up great stuff; you believe someday someone will start buying it. You won't improve the neighborhood. You let it go to seed because the money should just come in.

Figure out where your own attitudes are. Understand yourself as you go into this, your own ideas about money. You may or may not be able to avoid the pitfalls. But you might be better able to dig yourself out of the pit if you fall.

In Conclusion

These are the three things you need to remember about income and how it flows to an artist/writer:

- Money trickles in. It probably won't come all at once, in a deluge.
- The more sources that money trickles in from, the better.
- Understanding your own attitudes about money will go a long way toward helping you manage it when it does start coming in.

CHAPTER FOUR

Intuitive Budgeting

On certain topics, I am a contrarian.

I believe this is, in part, because I am an artist. In order for me to be able to do my art when society tells me I can't/shouldn't, I have to be able to tell society exactly which bridge they can jump off of.

Budgets are one of those hot spots for me.

If you tell me I *must* go on a budget, I will—not consciously, but unconsciously—break something, so that I can no longer stay on a budget.

I am a rational person. I understand budgets are good things.

For me, and for other artists that I know, budgets are worse than straitjackets. Just the thought of having a budget will drive them (and me!) crazy.

However.

I am also a professional. I run more than one business. I need to know what money is coming in and where it's going out.

So I have developed what I call *intuitive budgeting*: a way of understanding my cash flow and being able to make corrections without having to put myself on a budget.

By the end of this chapter, you should have some ideas for how to set up your own intuitive budgeting system.

Why Budget?

One of the things people don't tell you is *why* you need to budget. You don't, actually.

What you need is *a* budget. That is, you need to know how much money you're making, as well as spending, over a particular period of time.

Why do you need to know this?

So you can make adjustments as necessary. As things change, and drips accumulate, or perhaps dry up, you need to be aware and adjust.

You don't need to give yourself only X amount of money to spend on coffee every month.

You do need to know how much you're spending on coffee every month, and make adjustments if necessary.

Automation

If you are just starting off trying to figure out your finances, I would recommend reading with *I Will Teach You To Be Rich* by Ramit Sethi. His audience is twenty- and thirty-year-old people who have their first paychecks coming in; he tells them what to do with those paychecks. He writes in a very casual style that's very readable.

Fair warning—he also calls people idiots. This is not a guide for someone who is overly sensitive and needs a lot of handholding. He expects his readers to be smart. I found the book very refreshing.

I also discovered that I was already doing 99% of what he suggested.

I *luuurrrve* the internets and the modern day we live in. I take full advantage of as much automation as I possibly can in terms of my money.

What do I mean by automation?

If you are working for a regular company, chances are, your paychecks are automatically deposited into your account. If you're selling your work regularly through the usual distribution channels (Amazon.com, BarnesandNoble.com, Kobobooks.com, etc.) you're having those checks automatically deposited into your account.

This is automation that those companies have put in place regarding what they pay out.

You can set up the same sort of automation for yourself and the bills you pay.

If you own a house, your mortgage is probably automatically deducted. Maybe your heat and other utilities as well.

But wait! That's just money flowing in and out. No accountability.

Don't worry. This is just the start. Now let's dig into more details.

Alerts

Every credit card, as well as most banks, are happy to email you information about your accounts on a regular basis.

For example, you now have a credit card that's dedicated to your writing business. There won't be a lot of charges on it. One of the ways to track that card is to have the credit card company email you every time there's a charge made to that card.

This helps protect you against fraud—particularly when you get an email as soon as charges are made (and you didn't make them!).

I also have the credit card people send me an email every morning with my balance. This way, I know exactly what is on every card.

But how does this help you keep track of your spending?

Balances

I keep receipts. But I also buy 99% of everything using cards.

Most credit cards, and possibly your bank if you're using a debit card, have calculators—pie-charts—that show you where you've spent your money that month.

Instead of telling myself that I only have a specific amount of money to spend on something, I track at the end of the month (or, for me, more realistically, the end of each quarter) and see what I *have* been spending my money on.

By doing this sort of "after the fact" budget, of seeing what I was *actually* spending money on, I've been able to keep on track in terms of not spending more than I'm making.

For example, it became very clear at the end of one quarter, that I was spending way too much money at coffee shops. Because I could see my spending patterns, I was able to make changes.

Cash

This system of automating everything works if you use credit cards for everything, and you pay them off completely at the end of every month. (Me, I'm pathological about debt. I have none. Your mileage may vary—YMMV.)

But what if you use cash for everything? I understand that level of paranoia, of not wanting to pay off a large bill at the end of every month.

Then you must keep receipts. And then you must enter them into a program like Quicken or Quickbooks.

I know, I know. Not very intuitive.

However, cash is one of the easiest ways to lose track of your money.

You may think you have better control of your cash. And possibly you do, if you only spend cash on specific items.

But chances are, you spend cash on a lot of things. And you don't track your receipts. So you lose track of where you are and you end up in a hole.

I know too many artists who get into holes and then end up digging a deeper one.

Accounting

At the end of every quarter, I put all of my expenses into an accounting program. I've used GnuCash, but have now switched over to Quicken.

Since I've used credit cards for everything, it's very easy to enter receipts and assign my expenses to the correct category.

I know people who do this every week. I can't. I tried. Too much like a budget.

Instead, I buy a nice bottle of wine at the end of every quarter that I don't allow myself to open until I put in my receipts. (Carrots work *much* better than sticks for some artists.)

I can see that bottle of wine sitting there, unopened on my counter, every day, until I go ahead and enter in my receipts.

Online Programs

You can also use an online program, like Mint.com, for tracking your money. They have great charts showing you where you spent everything. You can download the reports to automatically enter into your own accounting software. Etc.

The problem? I have to give them the password for my bank account. And my credit card account.

How secure are they? You hear about companies being hacked all the time.

Do I want all of those passwords stored on a site I don't control?

Maybe it's fine. Maybe they're never hacked. Or maybe you're willing to take the risk.

It's up to you, how you track your money.

But you can't make adjustments to your spending, which is all about what a budget is supposed to be used for, if you don't know what things you're spending your income on.

In Conclusion

These are the three things you need to remember about intuitive budgeting:

- The purpose of a budget is to track your money so you can make adjustments if necessary.
- Use automation, such as emails from your credit cards or bank, to help you keep track of everything. Also use the online tools provided by your bank or credit card to determine in which categories you're spending too much money.
- Enter your receipts into an accounting program from time to time. Some people do it weekly. I do it quarterly.

Others do it annually. But you must keep track of how much you're spending, and where, so you can make adjustments.

CHAPTER FIVE

Income vs. Profit

So you've sold a story to a major short story market. Congratulations!
   Quick quiz: Is that income? Or profit?
   This chapter discusses the differences between income and profit, as well as delves further into expenses you can expect to incur.

Income

   The above is actually a trick question.
   The money from a sale may be income.
   It may be profit.
   The difference between income and profit are your expenses.
   Income is all the money that comes in to the writer, generally from licensing rights to your property (remember, though we always talk about *sales*, we, as artist/writers, aren't actually selling stories).
   Every drop, every trickle, every stream is considered income that comes into a writer's money bucket.

Expenses

Expenses are made up of the money you spend to run your business.

For example, paying for the services of a copyeditor is a normal business expense for a writer.

If you are publishing your own work, you may pay for a cover. That is another normal business expense.

Perhaps you have a website. The annual expense of registering that domain and paying for web hosting are normal business expenses.

Expenses take money out of the bucket of income.

NOTE: Be careful how much you spend out of that bucket if not a lot is trickling in! Spending $5000 on a short story cover and advertising makes no sense.

Profit

Profit is what remains of your income after you subtract your expenses.

So you have income, which is money flowing *into* the bucket.

Expenses are things you purchase for your business, which means money flowing *out of* the bucket.

Profit is what remains in the bucket *after* the expenses.

Think about your subdivision of properties.

You need to water the yards there. Or paint the houses. Or build new houses.

All of these are expenses that you spend out of your income.

Businesses are always trying to find legal ways to maximize income and minimize profit.

Why?

Taxes.

The less profit you have, the lower your taxes may be.

Again, I am not a tax professional and I am not giving you tax advice.

However, if you have enough legitimate expenses from your business, you may be able to lower all of your taxes.

Accounting

So, in the last chapter, I talked about intuitive budgeting.

The whole *income vs. profit* is why you must keep your receipts, and why you must keep track of everything you spend for your business, and possibly for your life.

What sort of expenses do you need to keep track of?

- Website domain
- Email forwarder (from your domain to your regular email address)
- Privacy service on your domain registration*
- All editing
- Cover artwork and design
- Writing computer (more about this in *The Physicality of Writing* chapter)
- Office equipment, such as your computer, a printer, your standing desk, etc.
- Postage (if you're mailing manuscripts to editors)
- Scans of signed contracts
- General supplies, like pens, paper, Post-it notes, etc.
- Software used specifically for writing and publishing
- Backup devices

SIDE NOTE: All domain registration information is public information. Which means that your name, address, and phone number are all easily accessible if you do not purchase a privacy service from your web host.

You may want to set up a home office and declare that on your taxes. The rules are fairly strict, however, about separating your business and personal activities in your home and what percentage of the space can be deducted, so be careful. The rules can be found on the IRS site about business expenses.

In Conclusion

These are the three things you need to remember about income vs. profit and expenses:

- Income is the money that flows to the writer.
- Expenses are the services or supplies you purchase for running your business. Be careful with your expenses.
- Profit is what remains after you subtract your expenses from your income.

CHAPTER SIX

Communication

In the previous chapters, I've been talking a lot about setting up your business and running it.

This is the transition chapter. The focus will be shifting from business to writing. There will still be talk about business; you are a professional, after all. But instead of just business, it's more the business of writing.

I personally have not always had a supportive partner in my writing career. I have always tried to maintain a good social network. Writers do tend to flock together.

This chapter is about those people affected by your writing business—family, partners, spouse, friends—and communicating with them.

The Partner

I am currently blessed with a tremendously supportive partner. This hasn't always been the case in my life.

I've talked with too many artists/writers who do not have supportive partners, spouses, wives, husbands.

If you are going to survive as an artist, not to mention reach your full potential, your partner *must* be supportive. Not merely tolerant, and absolutely not hostile.

Supportive.

Chances are, if your partner isn't an artist or creative in ways similar to you, they don't understand what's going on with you. Why you're still working even if you're staring out a window. How even asking, "Is there anything you need?" can be horrifically disruptive.

However, it is up to *you* to communicate.

Can you read minds? I know I write about people who can, but honestly, truly, I can't.

Neither can your partner.

You *cannot* assume that they know what's going on with you. You have to use your words to let them know.

You're a writer. Send them an email if you can't tell them in person.

But you must tell them. You must communicate that this is important to you. That you need this time.

It isn't a one-way street. Make sure they know that as well.

You will need to negotiate. If you get two hours in the evening alone to write, maybe you get up an hour early to get the kids ready for school so your spouse can sleep in.

Maybe you get to do the dishes all alone every night. I've always found that doing things like dishes are a good time to plot, as long as no one disturbs me. So you promise that the kitchen will always be clean, you'll always do the dishes, as long as you get to do them alone.

There are ten thousand different compromises and negotiations you can make with your partner.

Make them. And keep working on them. Check in monthly to make sure that things aren't sliding. That the deals you've arranged are still working.

Communicate.

Co-Conspirator

Unindicted, of course.

Are there things your partner is good at? Perhaps she has a head for money and is frustrated by your lack of budget.

Maybe your partner writes good ad copy.

Or maybe your partner has always wanted to learn how to create a website.

You won't know until you ask. There may be things that he or she would like to help with, but they don't know how to ask, either.

If they express interest in your business, see if there are ways they can help.

Maybe they don't want to write, but they'd love to brainstorm with you.

Maybe they can be a first reader, or a copy editor. Or something else.

Bring them along for the journey.

This doesn't have to be a trip for one.

Communicate.

Bulletproof

Diving off the cliff into the great unknown of the creative world can be scary.

Publishing a novel, putting it up for the whole world to see, can be frightening.

You may not be worried about these things. But there are things that do worry you about this business. What if the current distribution systems fail? What if royalties fall? And so on.

Be sure to share not only your work, but your fears with your partner.

You should *not* be bulletproof, not about your business, not with your partner.

They need to know that you are scared about this. Chances are, they're frightened as well. Unless you can communicate your fears to them, they may never be able to tell you their fears.

You'll never be able to share and support each other if you don't talk about your fears.

Discussing your fears will bring your partner closer to your business.

Communicate.

Network

You may not have a partner or co-conspirators. I didn't for years. I still maintained a network.

If you live in a city, it won't be that difficult to find other writers, artists, creative types. It may be difficult finding other *professional* writers, but that's a different matter.

If you don't live in an urban area, there are virtual groups and networks you can create and maintain.

Why are networks important?

Networks provide opportunities. Not for other people to help you, but for you to help other people. (You do realize that's why you network, right? So you can find opportunities to help someone else?)

Writing is a solitary exercise. Even if you're writing with a group, sitting around a table in a coffee shop, the story is still taking place between your ears.

Having a network and other people to support you is essential for your continued health as a writer/artist. People who can speak the same language. Maybe they aren't writers. Maybe they're musicians. Or painters. However, they share that same *spark*.

The best writers are only partially hermitish. When they can, they spend time with other people, out of their own heads.

Your network will help you get out. They'll help you find ways to help other writers or artists. Always pay it forward.

Maybe at some point, there will be a time when the people in your network can turn around and help you.

Communicate with them as well.

In Conclusion

Here are the three things you need to remember about communications:

- Your partner doesn't know what's going on with you. You must communicate.
- You can't be bulletproof. Share your fears as well as the work and the joy.

- It doesn't matter if you have partners or not. You should still develop a network of other artists and writers.

CHAPTER SEVEN

Self-Confidence 101

I'm a fairly confident person. I've been teased about being a Towering Mountain of self-confidence.

However, I'm also a completely neurotic artist as well as an introvert.

How did I get this self-confidence? I certainly wasn't born with it. It's something I worked at.

This chapter is about you, the artist/writer, achieving some level of self-confidence.

Travel

When I was in my early thirties, I bought a one-way ticket to Europe. I had no idea when, or even if, I would return to the United States.

I ended up traveling around the world for three-and-a-half years, working and traveling.

About halfway through the trip, I ended up in Tainan, Taiwan, teaching English at an after-school cram school.

I had been traveling for almost a year and a half. I had worked on an archaeological dig in Yorkshire, England. I had taught English as a second language in Budapest, Hungary. I had taken the trans-Siberian railroad from Budapest to Moscow, then all the way across Russia to Beijing. I had traveled through China by myself for a month, before making my way to Hong Kong, and then Taiwan.

I had done all of these things, and yet, I was convinced I was a failure.

I didn't travel like other people. I must have been doing it wrong. I was failing at *traveling*.

I spent a day out on a pier, sitting over the ocean, having a talk with myself. I compared the reality of what I had done with how I was judging myself.

The two weren't even on the same planet.

I was not failing at travel. I was not a failure. I was just marching to my own drummer, traveling at my own speed, carving my own path to the mountain. I wasn't following in anyone else's footsteps.

And that was okay.

That was when I figured out—and the lesson sank deep into my bones—that the only failure was to *not* do. To not travel. To not try new things.

To not write.

Reality

While I encourage every single one of you to go travel, I don't believe that you have to go to the extremes that I did to gain more self-confidence.

You need to use the same trick I did, though.

That is, you need to compare the actual reality of what you're doing to your judgment about it.

Ready?

Do you write? Do you actually commit words to a page?

If so, congratulations! You are now in the top one-and-a-half percentile of all writers.

The majority of people who want to be writers merely talk about it. They plan on writing someday. They'll get around to it.

Just the fact that you write makes you special. Different.

Do you finish what you write?

Hallelujah!

That puts you in the top percent of the top percent. There is a large subsection of writers who never finish what they write.

Those two accomplishments, by themselves, should give your self-confidence a boost. You're doing something amazing, that most people honestly can't do, and never will.

You write.

That makes all the difference in the world.

Judgment

I can hear you, you know.

Yeah, that's easy to say. But everything I write is crap!

Writers are the worst judge of their own work. I know New York Times bestsellers who have sold millions of books, who get fans lined up around the block when they do a signing, who firmly believe that everything they write is crap.

Michael Connolly felt that he wrote crap. His wife was the one who rescued his first manuscript and sent it off.

You cannot judge your own work.

But—

No. You, the writer, don't know what you write.

You cannot judge it.

First Readers

What you need is a good first reader.

Not a critique group.

It's all about intent.

I can critique anything. I can critique Pulitzer Prize winning novels. I can critique Hugo Award winning short fiction.

The *intent* of critique is to tear apart. Generally you get critique from other writers. Or from your own inner critic.

A *reader's* intent is to enjoy a good story. They won't care about perfect grammar, they won't care about metaphors. They certainly won't attack your work. They just want a good story.

So instead of a critique group, find readers. Preferably readers who read a lot and like to read. (This can be how you bring in your partner, your friends, your coworkers, as part of your support network, as mentioned in a previous chapter.)

Readers won't critique. They might say, "I didn't believe this guy when he said X." Or they'll say, "I couldn't finish it." Or maybe they'll say, "Where's the next chapter?"

A reader won't know *how* to fix something. They can just point out *where* you may need to fix things.

But...

No, really. You need to be able to show your work to readers.

Why are you writing? It may be that you are writing only for yourself, that you never intend to show your work to others.

If that is the case, that's awesome. Go you! But you need to own that. You need to declare it to your partner, to your support network.

You need to truly believe that intent, deep down in your bones.

If, however, your intent is to *sell* your work, you need to be able to show it to readers.

Perhaps the first reader you find isn't the right one. Not every reader loves every work. Think about yourself as a reader. Do you love Stephen King and buy everything he writes in hardback? Or would you not touch his work with a ten-foot pole?

All readers are like that. They have their own tastes and preferences.

Keep looking. You'll find a reader. You'll find *your* reader. The one who loves your work and always points out the one spot that you knew deep in your bones needed to be fixed. Or perhaps you'll find several, one for every genre you write in.

You can also train your reader. Ask them leading questions *after* they've read your work. (Never prejudice a reader with things to look for *before* you hand them your work.) Ask if they believed this character, if they liked the setting here, was it magical enough, did it make sense.

Believe

You must *believe* your reader when she tells you, "This is great! Send it out!"

Sometimes, the hardest thing for a writer to hear is praise.

We know how to work hard. *What do you mean, I don't need to work on this piece anymore?* It makes no sense.

Believe your first reader. Believe in yourself. Believe that you can write.

In Conclusion

Here are the three things you need to remember about self-confidence:

- Do a reality check. Without the judgment.
- You're writing and finishing what you write. This sets you far beyond most people who say they want to write.
- Share your work with first readers, not a critique group.

CHAPTER EIGHT

Writing Comes First

I was in my mid-thirties before I made a serious commitment to my writing.

Oh, I was always writing. And finishing short stories. And sending them to magazines (and getting rejected!).

But in my mid-thirties, something clicked. I found a story (or that story found me) and was dragged into it. I *had* to write every day. The story demanded it.

Then I found another story. And another.

And I realized that before, while I'd claimed to be a writer, the writing wasn't that important. Many, *many* other things came first.

If you want to be a professional writer, the writing must come first.

In this chapter, I talk about some ways to help you put the writing first.

The Early Years

When I first made the commitment to my writing, I felt as though I was being very harsh. I judged *everything* in my life: the day job, the boyfriend, my other friends, my working out, my cat, everything.

I looked at every piece of my life and asked one simple question: *Does this support the writing?*

If so, great!

If not, I jettisoned it.

Then I went through the whole process again, six months later. And again, six months after that.

It was a time of great purging for me. I lost friends. But they weren't really friends, not if they made fun of my writing, or didn't understand that I couldn't go out with them that night because I was writing.

This is tied directly to self-confidence. I hadn't sold anything. I was still trying to figure out what it meant to be a writer.

But I had the self-confidence to put the writing first. This is why the chapter on self-confidence comes before this one.

You must believe in yourself. A supportive spouse is awesome, particularly one who won't let you quit after your two-hundredth rejection. But you may not have a spouse. You have to believe in yourself. Do it on your own.

WIBBOW (pronounced "wih-bow")

Scott William Carter is the one who originated this acronym. It's a great yardstick for measuring all the other activities that people tell you that you *must* do, like talking with fans on Facebook, like doing a blog tour, like setting up a signing.

It stands for:

Would I Be Better Off Writing?

There is one piece of marketing that works for all writers, in all genres, to increase sales:

Writing and publishing the next book.

You'll see a bump in sales of previous books when you release the next book. Particularly in a series. (It's all part of that slow and steady drips to trickles to streams to rivers.)

So when someone asks you to do something, fall back to WIBBOW.

Would I be better off writing the next book, the next chapter, the next story?

It's less harsh than my original question, but just as important.

Most of the time, when you've reached a situation where you have to ask this question, the answer is *yes*, I would be better off writing.

There are times when the answer is *no*. For me, I've found it has to do with relationships and family. Sometimes someone needs me and it's better for me to be with them.

Honestly though, 99% of the time, when I ask myself if I'd be better off writing, the answer is *yes*.

How?

So how do you make the writing come first? How do you consistently answer *yes* to WIBBOW?

As I mentioned before, you have to have some level of self-confidence. Your writing is important to you. You are important to you. So put it first.

What does that mean?

Turn off the TV. I got rid of my TV years ago. When I want to watch something, I can always watch it on my computer.

Remember—you are a creator of content. Consuming content is not creating.

Stop reading blogs. I will admit that I still get sucked into reading a lot of blogs, tech blogs and business blogs and writing blogs. I've had to delete the app that I use to keep track of sites more than once.

Get off Facebook and social media. I know, I know. It's a party out there, and you're afraid you're going to miss something.

In a year from now, when you look back, would you rather have watched the latest viral video ten times or written another novel?

Negotiate time for yourself. If you're living with someone, you need to communicate with them about your needs. They can't support you if they don't know that you need this time to write. Don't get angry at them for disturbing you if you haven't explained just how important this time is.

This can include negotiating with your boss at your day job as well. As far as my day job was concerned, I had a "life conflict" early in the morning, every morning, and couldn't attend early-morning meetings. The boss doesn't need to know that's your writing time—make up a story about kids or your spouse or your parents or whatever. (Unless you have a supportive boss, which is awesome.)

Get a different job. Seriously, if you're working sixty-plus hours a week and are having difficulty writing because you're mentally exhausted all the time, find a different job. I know that's difficult. It isn't impossible.

How badly do you want to write? How strong is your hunger? How much do you want it?

I negotiated a thirty-hour-a-week deal for the day job, taking a pay cut, so I could write in the mornings.

The writing comes first.

In Conclusion

Here are the three things you need to remember about the writing:

- The writing comes first. Jettison those things that don't support that.
- WIBBOW. *Would I be better off writing?* Most of the times, the answer is yes.
- Purge what you can, so when you look back in a year, you'll have another novel, not a bunch of Facebook "friends."

CHAPTER NINE

This Is The Schedule...For Now

Schedule.

I *hate* that word. Hate it anytime I have to be on one.

A schedule is one of those hot buttons for me, as well as for a lot of other artists that I know.

Being on a schedule will drive us crazy. It isn't how we want to live.

I will make a deadline. That's different. I'm a professional.

But the rest of the world works on schedules.

This chapter talks about how, as an artist, you can approach schedules that the rest of the world demands and make them work for you.

Time

One of the best things in the world about writing full time is that I don't have to get up at the same time every day.

That may seem strange to some of you. But for me, and for other artists I know, getting up at the same time every day is hard. It grates against my soul. That's the only way I can think to describe it.

I believe it has to do with the difference between being *time driven* and *event driven.*

Time-Driven

In a time driven world, you get up at 5:15 a.m. every day. You shower, shave, drive into work. Have breakfast and coffee there. Read the news. Go through your email. And start writing every morning at 7 a.m.

Everything is done according to a clock.

If this kind of thing works for you, great.

If this is the only way you can find the time for writing, also good.

But for a lot of writer/artists, this sort of regimented, time-based schedule will only work for a very short while. Then the writer will burn out on the schedule. They can no longer be productive, and they may or may not understand why.

Event-Driven

Instead of getting up at a specific time every day, I get up when I wake up, generally sometime between 6 a.m. and 8 a.m. (I do have an alarm set for 7 a.m.) I walk for a mile or more every morning to wake up. When I come home, I feed the cat (because she's convinced she's starving).

Then I write. I finish the scene or chapter or what have you, go take a shower, then go back and write some more.

Only after I've finished two writing sessions do I eat breakfast, open my email, let the world in.

This is my habit. I've made it a strong habit, such that it feels bad when I don't follow this.

Notice that my day is *not* time driven. There are no times associated with any of the events. One just follows the next. Maybe I take only thirty minutes to write. Maybe I take three hours. I don't know, and I don't have to plan it. It just happens.

There's actually some research exploring how "clock-time" people are less creative than "event-time" people (*Journal of Personality and Social Psychology*, June 2014).

The Reality

Most artists don't have the luxury of being full-time creatives. They need that day job and that paycheck.

Or perhaps they live with a partner, or have a family. They have other demands that they must meet, and that includes being on a schedule, being time-driven.

The rest of the world marches to a clock. As an artist, you have to at least fake it.

Negotiate. Then Re-negotiate.

If it's possible, get your partner or family or support network or whoever it is that is in your life to understand that the schedule you negotiate with them is *temporary*.

Not because you want it to be. Not because you're a flaky artist.

But because the schedule won't always work for you.

Schedules will work for a while. How long depends on the schedule and your temperament. For me, I've always found a schedule may work for two to three months. Sometimes four. But generally no longer than that.

Then I'm no longer productive. And the schedule grates on me so hard my teeth ache. It's awful. And I feel awful.

But the writing comes first. So I re-negotiate the schedule. Change things around.

Work with the knowledge that no schedule will ever be permanent.

Build Habits

As I mentioned above, I don't have a schedule, not really.

I have *habits*.

For example, instead of writing at 7 p.m. every night after dinner, I merely write after dinner.

That gets me out of the false trap of, "Well, it's 7:10. I've missed my writing time. Oh well!"

I write after dinner, whether that be 6:30 p.m. or 8 p.m. It's a habit: event driven, not time driven.

Animals

Do you have a cat or dog or some other faithful companion? You might think they're time driven, but really, for the most part, they're event-driven.

My partner comes home generally around 5:30. My cat gets fed at 5 p.m.

Sometimes my partner comes home early, occasionally as early as 4:30. The cat is *convinced* that I've forgotten to feed her. The events haven't happened in the right order.

I've recently gotten into the habit of brushing my cat every morning, some time after I shower. Again, it doesn't matter what time it is to her. I've showered and dressed. It must be time for her brushing.

But Then There's The Day Job...

And the day job demands a time frame that's pretty rigid. You can't escape it. It grates, but you need to eat.

There's not much you can do about that kind of schedule. It's imposed on you and you can't really escape (unless you change jobs, or start working for yourself).

To survive, I've always built habits around those hours. If you write best in the morning, give yourself an extra thirty-minute timeframe for getting up so you don't have to stick to the same time every day.

If you write best in the evenings, again, let yourself mix it up as much as you can. Maybe you eat dessert first, then write, then have dinner. Or maybe you walk every night after work to get in some movement. Walk to a coffee shop to write. Or jog there.

Keep the rest of your life as fluid as you can. It will help you survive the rest of the schedule. If you try to schedule your writing like the rest of your life, you'll burn out.

In Conclusion

Here are the three things you need to remember about schedules:

- Many artist/writers are event-driven, not time-driven. Build habits around events, not hours on the clock.
- Change your schedule when it stops working for you. Don't be surprised if that's every other month.
- Keep your personal schedule as fluid as possible if you have a rigid work schedule.

CHAPTER TEN

The Physicality Of Writing

Most writing takes place between your ears. You play head games with yourself and your characters.

But writing is also a physical act. If you're dictating your words, it's less so. More so, though, if you're typing.

This chapter addresses some of the physicality of writing.

Separate Computer

As I've mentioned in a previous chapter, I build habits. Habits help me write more, better, faster.

One of the things I've done to encourage my writing habit is to get a separate writing computer.

Every time I sit down at this computer, the only thing I can do is write.

There is no internet connection on this computer. There are no games. There is a word processor and a spreadsheet program. That's it.

I got this computer fairly cheaply online, refurbished.

Some people don't work well with a second computer, or they can't afford the expense. Instead, they've set up a second user on their primary computer.

That user has no access to the internet. No access to games or anything other than their word processor.

This way, when the writer signs in with this dedicated writing account, they are creating the habit and setting the expectation that it's time to write now.

Some have even gone so far as to have a different image on their computer background as well as a different screen saver for that user, so that when they sign in with this user, there are visual cues that it's time to write.

No Internet

But I just need to look up this one thing…

Then it's two or three hours later and there aren't any words on the page.

Some people use "Write or Die." Or maybe they have a program that throws kittens at them when they complete so many words.

If I relied on that type of external reward for writing, I'd burn out. As a full-time professional, my motivation and rewards *must* come from inside me, and not be external.

So again—no internet. It disturbs the flow of the creative voice. Trust me on this one.

RSI

Those three dreaded letters: RSI. Repetitive Stress Injury.

Basically, it means doing the same action over and over again until you've injured yourself.

Friends have likened RSI to feeling as though knives were being thrust into their wrists every time they tried to type.

This really interferes with the writing, you know?

But RSI is not inevitable. There are things you can do to help prevent getting an RSI.

Breaks

You've started writing. You're in the flow. Now I expect you to take breaks?

Yes.

Again, typing or writing things out by hand is a physical activity. You need to take breaks. No matter if you're in the flow or not. Start teaching yourself to take breaks every hour.

For those who handwrite, use a timer. Take a break every hour. Get up, stretch, etc.

If you're on a computer, I recommend workrave.org for those on PCs and dejal.com/Timeout for those on Macs.

I have mine set to give me a thirty-second break every twenty minutes, then at fifty-five minutes to take a five-minute break.

The workrave.org program also gives you stretches.

When I started using these programs, I labeled them my 'productivity software'.

By taking regular breaks, I'm able to work more hours during the day. I'm also able to work harder, because I know that a break is coming.

So take breaks. Your body and your mind will thank you for it.

Stretches

When you take your five-minute break every hour, one of the things you should do is stretch.

If you do an internet search for "RSI Stretches," you'll find a lot of advice. Most of what I've seen, though, doesn't cover enough. Merely stretching your wrists and hands isn't good enough.

Some of the muscles that need stretching are in your armpit. Raise your hand over your head and place it on a wall, then lean into it gently. This will stretch those muscles.

Be sure to also stretch out the muscles across your chest. And your neck and shoulder muscles.

Ergonomic

I use a combination of boxes and computer stands in order to achieve an ergonomic desk arrangement with my laptop and keyboard. For me, it's all about looking up and not looking down while I'm working. My neck and back seem to be more sensitive to incorrect posture than my wrists and shoulders. At least for now.

Do what you can to get your monitor raised so you're looking up. Your hands and wrists supported. Your keyboard at the proper height.

Again, see if you can get refurbished equipment somewhere, so you'll have the right stuff that works for you and will help prevent injuries.

You're in this for the long haul. That means keeping your body in shape.

Standing

I actually stand most of the time when I write. There are times when I sit. I find that I sit when I'm writing close, intimate scenes. But when I'm writing scenes with a lot of action, standing works better.

It took some training for me to be able to stand when I wrote. I know it isn't for everyone. But I feel so much better when I spend the day standing instead of sitting.

You don't have to get the top-of-the-line standing desk. You can jerry-rig something. Then maybe after your first best seller, you treat yourself to a proper standing desk.

But try it. You may like it.

Treadmills

I, personally, am not steady enough to walk and write. I'm also not "there" enough when I'm writing. The rest of the world completely disappears and I'm afraid I'd hurt myself if I tried walking and writing.

But I know some writers who swear by their treadmill desk. Claim it makes them more productive. More creative.

There have been many studies showing that movement will improve your creativity. So I believe the writers who say they can do this.

Again, you can always redneck something that works for you.

There are people who dictate their writing while they're walking. This way, they're not limited to a treadmill, but can take a hike and still write. I'm not to that stage yet, but I have considered it.

In Conclusion

Here are the three things you need to remember about the physicality of writing:

- Separate your writing space from your regular workspace. This helps build the habit and expectation that all you're going to do is write when you go there.
- Stretch and take breaks.
- Try to write standing up, or even walking. You may be surprised at the results!

CHAPTER ELEVEN

What's Stopping You From Writing?

I love to write. I love making stuff up, from world to characters to crises. There's no better feeling in the world than finishing that car chase or long story arc. I feel like I need a cigarette sometimes.

And yet, like most writers, I sometimes have problems getting myself to the chair. It's all in my head, and sometimes, that isn't the most pleasant place to be.

This chapter deals with some of the things that may be stopping you from writing.

Wrong Turn

There are times when I'm cruising along, happy to be writing, and the words suddenly just grind down. Every sentence becomes excruciatingly difficult to write.

But I like this story! I like these characters! What's wrong?

I've learned that when the flow disappears, it's often because I've made a wrong turn somewhere upstream.

For example, a character goes into a room and ignores the door leading out, but instead, exits the same way she came in. About two pages later, I'll realize that the character needed to go through that other door instead.

I'll throw away everything from the point of the wrong turn and take the right turn instead.

Most recently, I realized I needed another scene with my main character earlier in the novel. The scene I was currently trying to write was actually that earlier scene.

My subconscious knows how to tell stories. If I'm stopping mid-scene and unable to write, it's because there's generally something wrong at the story level.

Messy Middle

Despite being a Towering Mountain of self-confidence, there are times while I'm writing a novel when I start to doubt myself. When I wonder if the story I'm telling is interesting to anyone who isn't me. When I worry that I've gone too weird, or too normal, or too…you get the idea.

If I can lift my head from the page and look at where I'm at, I'll eventually realize that I'm in what I call the "messy middle."

For some writers this happens in the first third of the novel, these huge moments of doubt.

For me, it's about halfway through.

I've written enough novels at this point to be able to identify that this is just a normal part of my process. I just have to push through the messy middle. The downhill slide to the end is just ahead, and it will be a race to the finish.

Project Block

I don't tend to get project block—that is, stopped in the middle of a project—for very long. If I've stopped, it's because of one of the two things above.

There are other writers I know who do get project block—they stop in the middle of a project and can't finish.

It may just be that they aren't ready to write that project yet.

For me, project block happens before I even start. I can try to build enthusiasm for a project, try to tell my inner writer how much fun this new thing will be.

She ignores me and goes off to do whatever she has planned.

There are projects that I can't write yet. I'm not ready, or the story isn't ready in my head.

So I switch to a different project.

Project selection is key for me. If I don't choose the right project, I can't write.

Choose the right project. Choose the one with the strongest "Oh!" factor, the one you think is coolest, the one that makes you giggle more.

Life Happens

There are times when you won't write. Every writer goes through these periods. Again, writing is all in our heads, and sometimes our heads just aren't right.

For example, I stopped writing for a couple of years after my mother died. I went through a tremendous number of changes at the time—lost my cat, my job, my house, got a divorce, moved, and lost my mom.

I was far too messed up emotionally to write.

I didn't have writer's block, however. I define writer's block as that time when you have words piling up and you want to write, but you're not able to. The words just won't come.

For me, at that time, there were no words.

I trusted that the words would come back. And they did. I did "prime the pump," as it were, with a bunch of writing exercises (Judy Reeves, *A Writer's Book Of Days*).

But sometimes life happens. You don't write. And that's okay. You will later.

Giggling

The second most important thing I've learned about writing full time is that I *must* be giggling while I'm writing fiction.

That doesn't mean that the plot is lighthearted or silly. It can be a very serious story with a high body count.

However, there must be something about the book that makes me giggle. Some aspect that just makes me laugh manically. This is what will draw me to the page even beyond my set writing schedule. These are the things that make me joyfully return to that project.

I firmly believe that giggling is part of my writing process. It isn't part of everyone's—for others, I know it's a deep sense of satisfaction at a job well done, particularly for difficult topics.

You need to find what drives you, then make sure that every project has ample opportunities to use that.

Fear

I am a fairly fearless person. However, even I've found that there are times when fear has stopped me from writing.

Generally I'll be typing away, and suddenly I find that I'm no longer in my office. I've wandered into the kitchen, maybe I'm standing in front of the refrigerator (the most dangerous appliance for anyone who works at home full time).

What I've learned to do is to check in with myself. Why did I stop writing? Why am I here? Did I really need a break? Am I honestly hungry? Or is something else going on?

Fears are endless. You think you've conquered one, and maybe you have, but then it sneaks in a backdoor wearing sunglasses and a fake tan.

You need to deal with your fears. Or else you'll find yourself stopping again and again.

There are times when I have to shut the door to my office, physically cutting myself off from the outside world and all those external voices, in order to keep writing, to keep creating, to not compromise my vision because someone, somewhere, at one point, told me I was too weird.

If you have a lot of problems with fears, if you can't clear out the mess in your head, you might want to go get professional help. That will also mess you up for a while, but sometimes these things are too big to work through on your own.

Use your fears if you can. Write about what scares you. Exorcise those demons.

Don't let them stop you.

In Conclusion

Here are the three things you need to look at when you stop writing:

- Do you have project block? Have you made a wrong turn? Are you in the messy middle? Figuring out why you're stopping is crucial.
- Sometimes life happens. You'll get back to the writing when you can.
- Deal with your fears. Being able to write is worth it.

CHAPTER TWELVE

Practice

One of the greatest concepts that was ever shared with me by Dean Wesley Smith was the idea of *practice*.

It's head-scratching that I wasn't practicing before Dean said something about it. It made sense to me the moment he started discussing it.

I think it's one of the best tools in a professional writer's tool box. This chapter discusses practice, the how's and why's.

What Do You Mean, Practice?

In every art, there's a certain level of practice involved. You try something new. You experiment with it. You try it again. Then you do it some more.

For example, the first time you sat down with a sketchpad and pencil, did you just start drawing everything that was around you? No. You started with simple shapes and moved onto more complicated figures.

You might draw pages and pages of eyes, trying to get the expression just right, perfect the shape, figure out how to make the eyelid look realistic.

Then you move onto noses, and do the same thing. Over and over again.

Writing is the same way. You keep trying something, over and over, until you get good at it.

That Next Level

One of the things that I *love* about writing is that there's always something new to learn. A new technique. A new way of describing something. A new voice to experiment with.

Do I always succeed when I go swinging for the fences? Heck no. I have stories that are completely broken, that will never see the light of day because they're so unrepairable. Whole novels, in fact.

But that doesn't stop me from trying.

No matter how good you get, you should always be growing as an artist.

If you stop growing, chances are you'll also stop selling. Maybe not right away. But your work will no longer be fresh, alive, vibrant. And that will show. You're phoning it in.

The greatest writers of our time, the most successful, are still practicing. Still experimenting. They aren't doing the same thing over and over again.

As a reader, you know when a writer has stopped trying.

Don't be that guy.

Keep reaching for new heights.

How To Practice

Perhaps I've convinced you that you should practice.

The next question, of course, is *how*.

Every writer is going to be different in how they approach this. I can only tell you my method. You'll need to adapt it for your own work.

I primarily practice in novels, not short stories. (Though sometimes I go pretty far off the rails with an experimental short story.)

I will pick some aspect of storytelling that I want to practice for a particular novel. I have a reminder board on my door that I write things on. Generally, I'll write whatever I'm practicing on that board, so I'll see it every day.

The practice for this book? *Small bites.*

A lot of the topics in this book are large, sprawling, and interconnected.

I practiced taking small bites. Breaking things up. Not just ideas, but sentences. Sections.

Keep everything bite-sized, so it'll be easy to swallow, digest, and learn.

For the novels, I've had a lot of different practices. For example, for more than one novel I've practiced cliffhangers—that is, how to end a scene or chapter with a bang, pushing the reader forward. For other novels, I've practiced Voice. I write voicey things. I've practice Voice to make sure that a piece has a clear, distinct, possibly over-the-top voice.

But then I discovered that I sacrificed other things when I focused so much on Voice. So I wrote a novel where the practice was Voice with Setting.

I've also practiced being weird, going over the top, making non-sympathetic characters understandable enough that the reader didn't mind them, and so on.

There are so many things you can practice.

The project I'm working on will suggest the practice. Then I just remind myself, before I start writing, of what my practice is. I let my back brain take care of the rest.

The Joy Of Practice

As I've mentioned before, I giggle—a lot—when I'm writing fiction.

What I've discovered is that I'm generally practicing the thing that makes me giggle. For example, I recently had a novel where my board read, "Dare to be weird."

I discovered that every time I stopped giggling, it was because I'd gone normal. I'd done the expected thing.

I needed to go back, throw away what I'd written, and go weird. Go big. Go strange.

My practice is intimately tied to my enjoyment of a piece. If I'm doing my practice well, I know the work is good, too.

What To Practice

I read for enjoyment. I don't just read to do research. I'm right now reading a lot of modern poetry.

I know a lot of writers who don't read for enjoyment—either the other words coming in messes them up, or they can't turn off their critical brain, or what have you.

I think it's important to be able to read for enjoyment. It's part of that whole, "I want to learn new techniques."

You might think that's a contradiction—how can I read for enjoyment while at the same time learning?

This is where Jack comes in.

Remember—writer here. Lots of different people in my head.

I picture Jack as a Jack Russell Terrier. He sits, patiently nosing along, while I read for fun.

His job? Point out the unusual.

I'll be reading along and suddenly Jack will jump up, trying to get my attention. There will be something different about what I just read, something he hasn't seen before. For example, in *The Queen's Gambit* by Walter Tevis, mostly Jack just went along for the ride until the very last chapter, midway through the climax.

Took me a while to realize that the entire book had been written using a particular sentence structure, but that right there, for those two paragraphs, the sentence structure had changed.

It was masterfully done.

Will I ever practice that? Perhaps. Maybe try it first in a short story.

It's amazing the things that Jack points out. And he enables me to be able to relax enough to enjoy reading.

So this is one of the ways I figure out what to practice. By reading for enjoyment, and finding new techniques.

Judging Your Practice

When can a writer accurately judge whether a piece is successful or not?

Trick question.

A writer can *never* tell. Only readers know.

As I said, I've experimented and failed. But it was good practice. I didn't "waste" that time. I learned something.

Remember, the only way to fail is to not try.

Do you let your "failed" experiments and practice pieces out into the public?

If your first reader says you should.

I have a couple of stories that I feel as though I failed with—I didn't achieve what I was trying for. I was practicing, and it's obvious, to me, that I didn't make it. I didn't reach what I wanted to reach.

These are some of the stories that sell the best.

I cannot judge my own work. I have to let my first reader, and readers in general, tell me if I succeeded or not.

So practice. Write and release, if your first reader thinks you can. Repeat.

In Conclusion

Here are the three things you should remember about practicing:

- All art requires practice. Writing is no different.
- You can practice *anything*. Voice. Character. Setting. Weirdness. Small bites. Whatever you want to get better at for that particular work.
- Let your first reader judge whether you've succeeded or not.

IN CONCLUSION...

Congratulations! You're on your way to becoming a professional writer, one who isn't just focused on writing and the words, but also on the equally important *business* of writing.

Maybe you've set up a DBA by now, created your separate systems for doing your business accounting. Maybe you've set apart some time to talk with your partner about this writing thing. Or maybe you've started pricing second computers, wanting your own writing computer (it is a business expense, you know...).

Being a professional also means acting like one. I'm not saying that you can't go to cons and cosplay. (Seriously. Half my life, I think, is cosplay. Only I'm playing at being a professional writer.)

It does mean conducting yourself in a business-like manner.

Let me put it this way: Do you like buying coffee from the loud-mouthed, opinionated freak who always wants to get into an argument with you? Do you actually want to spend time with them?

Or do you prefer your coffee from a quiet (potentially scowling) barista who won't do much more than ask what you're having and tell you how much it cost? Who acts like a professional?

There may be times when you need to speak up, topics you feel strongly about. Ideas that you must share, your readership be damned.

At the same time, though, you're polite to your fans. You giggle and *squeeeee* with them. You reply to inquires about guest appearances in a timely, polite manner.

Just because you may be dealing with an idiot doesn't mean you should call him that.

You don't have to be lawyer-stiff in a tie and suit (unless that's what turns you on).

You should remember that everything that happens outside your word processor and you—everything that isn't the words—is the business, and you must remember to behave in a professional, business-like manner.

Some writers have great political rants. More power to them. I also, as a reader, won't read them anymore because I'm so turned off by their politics or their rants in general. Think about that before getting very opinionated. You may lose readers by being unprofessional.

Your mileage may vary. I would caution you, however, to be that professional person.

So what's next?

For me, it's always about the next book. In the *Business For Breakfast* series, I think the next book is going to be called, "The Beginning Professional Publisher." If you're publishing your own work, that book will hopefully help you get to the next professional level.

I'm considering partnering with an IP lawyer and doing some contract books, including "Contracts for Writers" and "Contracts for Publishers".

I might also do a book called, "So You Want To Publish An Anthology" and books on other advanced publishing topics.

Not related to writing, I will also write a book about running a vacation rental. Just 'cause. Reasons.

So, in conclusion—Write. Submit. Publish. Be professional. And be awesome to one another.

See you 'round the breakfast table.

Leah

APPENDIX

Recommended Reading List

There are lots of good books out there. Here are some suggestions.

Cutter, Leah. *Business for Breakfast, Volume 2: The Beginning Professional Publisher. Knotted Road Press, 2015.*

Daily, Frederick W. *Tax Savvy for Small Business.* NOLO, 2013.

Fishman, Stephen. *The Copyright Handbook: What Every Writer Needs To Know.* NOLO, 2014.

Mancuso, Anthony. *Incorporate Your Business: A Legal Guide to Forming a Corporation in Your State.* NOLO, 2013.

Reeves, Judy. *A Writer's Book of Days: A Spirited Companion and Lively Muse for the Writing Life.* New World Library, 2010.

Rusch, Kristine Kathryn. *The Freelancer's Survival Guide.* WMG Publishing, 2013.

Sethi, Ramit. *I Will Teach You To Be Rich.* Workman Publishing Company, 2009.

In addition, I would recommend taking any of these workshops:
http://www.deanwesleysmith.com/online-workshops/
These lectures are pretty good, too:
http://www.deanwesleysmith.com/lecture-series/

READ MORE!

Be sure to pick up the other books in the Business for Breakfast series!

The Beginning Professional Writer
The Beginning Professional Publisher
The Beginning Professional Storyteller
The Intermediate Professional Storyteller
Business Planning for Professional Publishers
The Healthier Professional Writer
The Three Act Structure

ABOUT THE AUTHOR

Leah R Cutter writes page-turning, wildly imaginative fiction in exotic locations, such as a magical New Orleans, the ancient Orient, Hungary, the Oregon coast, rural Kentucky, Seattle, Minneapolis, and many others.

She writes literary, fantasy, mystery, science fiction, and horror fiction. Her short fiction has been published in magazines like *Alfred Hitchcock's Mystery Magazine* and *Talebones*, anthologies like *Fiction River*, and on the web. Her long fiction has been published both by New York publishers as well as small presses.

Find Leah's books here.

Follow her blog at www.LeahCutter.com.

Never miss a release!

If you'd like to be notified of new releases, sign up for my newsletter.

I only send out newsletters once a quarter, will never spam you, or use your email for nefarious purposes. You can also unsubscribe at any time.

http://www.leahcutter.com/newsletter/

Reviews

It's true. Reviews help me sell more books. If you've enjoyed this story, please consider leaving a review of it on your favorite site.

ABOUT KNOTTED ROAD PRESS

Knotted Road Press fiction specializes in dynamic writing set in mysterious, exotic locations.

Knotted Road Press non-fiction publishes autobiographies, business books, cookbooks, and how-to books with unique voices.

Knotted Road Press creates DRM-free ebooks as well as high-quality print books for readers around the world.

With authors in a variety of genres including literary, poetry, mystery, fantasy, and science fiction, Knotted Road Press has something for everyone.

Knotted Road Press
www.KnottedRoadPress.com

www.ingramcontent.com/pod-product-compliance
Lightning Source LLC
Chambersburg PA
CBHW061612220326
41598CB00024BC/3564